C000227566

# Finishing Touch

*By Richard van Maanen*

*Illustrations by Tommaso Chiarolini*

First published in Great Britain in 2020



Illustrations, Cover design and typesetting by Tommaso Chiarolini

Editing and publishing by UK Book Publishing

www.ukbookpublishing.com

ISBN: 978-1-913179-62-5

*INDEX*

*DEDICATION*

*This book is dedicated to my wife, Sue, and our daughters, Catherine and Elizabeth, who prayed for my safety.*

# INTRODUCTION

*You don't have to be mad, but...*

*INTRODUCTION*

*You don't have to be mad, but...*

*If your idea of fun is getting up in the early hours of the morning, having an invigorating shower, driving long distances, without any break, against the clock and finally ending up in some strange bar the following morning for a nightcap or two before heading to bed for a couple of hours, then read on.*

*If you relish the thought of the thrills and spills of taking a 50 or 60 year old car on such a journey and lying on your back on some damp tarmac, holding a torch in your mouth, desperately trying to secure a nut or bolt when the need arises, then stay with me.*

*If you are keen on taking part in a competitive rally to savour the sights and sounds experienced during some of the most notorious International Rallies and Road Races, which took place in the immediate post-war period, when the drivers had no such aids as power steering, four wheel drive and sat nav, and health & safety was not on the agenda, and "real" heroes were born, mostly of the amateur variety, with no advertising or sponsorship, then this book may appeal to your condition!*

My own personal interest in rallying relates to the motoring period just after the war, when cars were becoming increasingly accessible to the average man on the street, when new marques were coming to the fore and the car industry was generally looking up. There seemed to be an excitement amongst designers to produce flowing aerodynamic designs, without the availability of wind tunnels and computer programmes. Designs were being influenced by the European styling houses of the day, with the need for more chrome and exciting features to reflect the demands of the young Americans, who were influenced by the movie and music scenes of that period. It was a time when the whole world was recovering from the devastation of the Second World War and, despite fuel rationing and the difficulty of obtaining parts and materials, people wanted to start enjoying life once more. In particular, the British automobile industry was expanding to meet the demands of both the home market and, more importantly, in order to help the economy, it was encouraged to export.

By the mid-fifties many of the new marques had fallen by the wayside in favour of the more successful manufacturers, who had gained some notoriety by winning and doing well in racing and rallying, and had become more focused on forming larger and more efficient corporations. The immediate post-war period was arguably the most exciting and liberating time in the automobile industry, the like of which we will perhaps never witness again.

It may have been the trip undertaken shortly after finishing university, when I, and a handful of like-minded companions hired an old Bedford Army truck to travel around North Africa for a few weeks, which sparked my desire for adventure. It was no more than a couple of years later that I discovered that old cars could offer that same kind of adventure, closer to home, but without the need to put up a tent in some distant desert each night.

There are around half a dozen major retrospective historic rallies which take place each year, and which in some way capture the spirit of the classic car scene. These include the Mille Miglia, the Monte Carlo, the Alpine, the Liege-Rome, the Tour Auto, the Tulip and the Targa Florio. There are many other historic rallies taking place today, both in the UK and abroad, but those I have mentioned are considered to be amongst the most prestigious. Taking part in historic rallies can certainly shed the pounds, both physically and fiscally, but there is a great deal of fun to be had getting lost in some out of the way place, with no one in sight save for the odd cow or sheep, keeping cool, and then once back on the right track, blasting down an open road. The challenge is simply to beat the clock, regardless of what is thrown at the competitors in the shape of closed roads, mechanical failures, lost maps and wrong turns.

So, this book endeavours to give a little flavour or insight into taking part in some of the aforementioned historic rallies, which are certainly no picnic or an extravagant adventure holiday with an old car, but real, competitive road rallies, where the intervals between the controls are not there in order to see another museum or castle, but to grab a quick bite to eat and have a swig of water, before visiting the boys' room, so that no time might be lost during the next six hours of driving.

My accounts would have been rather bland if I were to say that we cleared all the stages, my car behaved faultlessly and we won many trophies in the process; to say we were never so much as a second outside our respective times, would be unrealistic. I am certainly no Stirling Moss and one of my motors is a standard 1954 car, with original equipment and specification, which meant I struggled to keep up with the speeds set by the organisers. Competing against more modern and, often, upgraded vehicles, my exploits were always going to be full of excitement and adversity.

Apart from recording my experiences during historic rallies, it has to be said that the main purpose of this book is to share my interest in the history of rallying and road racing immediately after the Second World War and also to offer some insight into what might be expected of new entrants to the rally circus, who have not had any first-hand experience of taking part in those significant Historic Retrospective Rallies. I hope that, having read about the rallies in which I have participated, others will be encouraged to give it a try with a little bit of forewarning.

To win any significant rally may give the victors some brief recognition in the historic rallying scene, and those who finish second may soon be forgotten. Therefore, it is imperative, when competing in these retrospective events, that we do not get too engrossed in achieving a result, which is very much dependent upon the type of vehicle you use, the originality or modified state of the vehicle, the regulations and handicaps imposed by the organisers and a great deal of luck. We are engaged in re-enacting a time in our motoring history, which has long since passed, a time when amateurs could mix it with the professionals and there was a camaraderie between entrants, which can often be missing in professional motorsport today. It is after all, not the winning that matters, but the taking part and most importantly the finishing!

# ALPINE

*The Ups and Downs of Rallying*

*ALPINE*

*Distance: 1,800 miles over 6 days*

*Austin Healey 100M*

The first International Alpine rally took place in 1929 as a conglomeration of the Swiss, Italian, German and Austrian automobile clubs. The first event started in Munich and ended on the shores of Lake Como, with some 80 entrants who travelled around 300 miles each day and stayed at the very best hotels each night, taking in such passes such as the Katschberg, Stelvio, Tauernpass, Loibl, Kreuzberg, Tyrracher Hohe and Pordoi Joch. The modern-day rally is set along remarkably similar lines.

Immediately after World War II, the French and the Italians were the first to get rallying underway again, with rallies and races reintroduced in 1947. One, in particular, was called the Coupe des Alpes organised by the Automobile Club de Marseille-Provence, which was also known as the Alpine Rally. During the 1950's and early 1960's, it was supported by various manufacturers to advertise their new models and to establish the great names of rallying. By the late 1960's, it was becoming increasingly harder to control the Alpine Rally due to the increase in tourist traffic in Austria and Switzerland. It was not until some 25 years later that the Rallye des Alpes was reintroduced in 1989, being along the same lines as the pre- and immediate post-war events, on the actual roads which the event had used in its heyday.

In 1953, Britain put forward more entries for the International Rallye des Alpes than any other country, except France, but without any notable success. Consequently, in 1954, five Austin Healey 100's travelled to Marseilles in the hope of achieving recognition in what was arguably the toughest road event in Europe. The route in 1954 was around 2,200 miles passing through France, Switzerland, Italy, Germany and Austria, over many famous passes, as previously mentioned. The average speeds for the class above 2,600cc generally ranged from 31mph to over 40mph on sections where the roads were temporarily closed by the local police. The most notable British effort in 1954 was that of Stirling Moss and John Cutts in a Sunbeam Talbot who were one of the 40 or so finishing teams. My reason for entering this event was, in some way, to recreate the spirit of the original event and to experience first-hand the difficulties of driving a standard Austin Healey 100, first registered in 1954, over some of the most challenging roads in Europe, immortalised in the Standard Motor Company and British Motor Corporation Films in period, which were narrated by Raymond Baxter.

In the year prior to my taking part, the Alpine Rally Association had set the average speed for the event at between 26 and 28 mph, with relatively short daily legs. You might therefore appreciate my trepidation when informed at the start of the year I was due to compete, which was my first experience of any such competitive rally, that the average speed was to be between 31 and 34 mph, not much different to that required in 1954, with very long daily legs and a total distance of around 1,800 miles over six days. It is accepted that, during 1954, the roads were not in quite as good condition as they are today, with many sections being over loose gravel, but, the cars used on the rally in 1954 were new and there was much less traffic, particularly in the more isolated regions. The contemporary event caters for all cars which would have competed in the original events, up to 1967, and therefore the organisers felt that a higher average speed would test the majority of the cars which were produced during the 1960's. An average speed of 31mph may well seem quite modest, but when negotiating and braking hard at hairpin after hairpin, on a steep incline, it soon becomes evident that it is no mean feat to maintain the pace. Indeed, it feels as though you are really pushing on.

Having entered the event, I entrusted the inspection and preparation of my car to an Austin Healey specialist, specifically requesting close inspection of the brakes. It was therefore with some astonishment, that when carrying out a final check of the vehicle myself, just before leaving for Geneva, that the shoe linings were found to be right down to the rivets and requiring immediate replacement. New linings were duly fitted, and a very pleasant journey was undertaken en-route to the scrutineering and start at Geneva.

It was of some concern that, during the scrutineering, the Volvo Amazon of one of the principal contenders for the event, caught fire and subsequently withdrew even before the send-off.

The sun was shining brightly on the first day, with speed tests during the afternoon over the Col du Grand St Bernard and the Col du Petit St Bernard, before an early evening dinner at Bourg St Maurice, where we made the passage control just minutes before our allocated time. After a hurried dinner lasting no more than 45 minutes, we were off for the breath-taking drive through and over the Val d'Isere, Col de L'Iseran and the Col du Mont-Cenis under the evening shadow of Mont Blanc, arriving at our final destination in Sestrière at around midnight. Driving the last part of the leg with full beam to light the road ahead, contending with one hairpin after another, was an experience I shall never forget, particularly one downhill hairpin section near Susa, when tiredness had set in and I was convinced that the road carried on straight ahead, when in fact it was a tight left hander. Luckily, I was able to react quickly and brought my car to an abrupt halt without going over the edge. Some time later, I was informed by the driver who had been a little further ahead of me, that he had also made the same misjudgement and had heard the squealing of my car brakes when he was further down the mountain.

After some four hours' sleep, we awoke the following morning at 6.30am and had soon commenced the long drive down to Marseille. It was with a degree of anxiety that, within a mile or so of leaving the morning control, high in the Italian Alps, I found my brakes required attention. Having stopped twice to adjust the brakes, it became necessary to pull up outside a bus garage in Briançon to remove the drums and thoroughly inspect the linings. To our horror the linings were more than fifty per cent worn and were suffering early fading, indicating that the recently fitted shoe linings were faulty. This unexpected delay meant that time was lost, and it was clear that we were unlikely to make the lunch control in Barcelonnette without cutting out some speed tests. We therefore decided to take a longer, but faster route, by-passing the Cols on the designated route, but were still five minutes outside our allocated time for arrival. Consequently, we had no lunch, just a swig of water before setting out on the afternoon navigational section over the Col d'Allos and the Grand Canyon du Verdun, finally arriving in the old Port of Marseille just after 8 pm, to a well-earned Black Tie dinner, which was held to commemorate the 100th anniversary of the Automobile Club de Provence.

We awoke at 6am the next morning, in good time to service the shoe linings and carry out general checks before our early start north to the famous Mont Ventoux, in glorious sunshine, passing the snow poles at the summit. It was, for us, more fun thrashing the car up the hill than down, due to the increasing fade we were experiencing with the linings. The morning stages involved navigation over some extremely poor single-track roads, which resulted in the front exhaust bracket coming away. Anyone familiar with Austin Healey 100's will know how low slung the car is. Mindful of the possibility of some clearance problems, I had fitted a new exhaust and brackets only a couple of weeks earlier and the new fittings provided an easy tied solution. However, just before the lunch control the rear exhaust bracket connection also came away, after we had erroneously gone down a particularly bad unmade road. Unfortunately, we were unable to tie the exhaust bracket effectively and, as a consequence, limped to the control some five minutes late of our allocated time. We checked out after a quick ten-minute lunch and headed out to look for a local garage for some urgent welding to the rear exhaust bracket. We found a small workshop in a farmyard, miles from anywhere, where the proprietor was more than happy to help us out, and we were most amused to see that sheep and chickens gathered around the mechanics while they were under our car carrying out the repair. As we looked around the yard, it became evident that this remote workshop was, in fact, used by the Peugeot Works Rally Team, with new cars in various stages of build under covers. We had clearly found the right place for a repair!

Once again, we faced high penalties if we failed to reach the final control in time and so a detour was made en-route to Albertville. Many cars were at this stage retiring, including the experienced team of Derek Skinner and Willy Cave, who had competed in the heyday of the event, in their Austin Healey 3000. Their car suffered a puncture and finally suspension failure.

On arrival at Albertville around 8.30pm, the very bright and hot sunshine gave way to the most spectacular thunderstorm over the Alps. This resulted in our having only 3-4 hours' sleep that night, before another early start the following morning, which saw us removing the drums again to clean the linings and adjust them for the arduous day ahead. As with the previous morning, the brakes performed satisfactorily over the first Col or so but soon faded thereafter. In an effort to minimise the wear on the linings, our braking was facilitated by using the gears and handbrake en-route, via St Gervais and Chamonix, to the first speed test of the day just past the Col de la Fordaz. We had achieved incredibly good results in all the speed tests, maintaining the prescribed average speed within 10 secs over a set distance of 10 miles or so.

The second speed test that day was a return to the Col du Grand St Bernard which, when climbing, was totally immersed in low cloud, but as luck would have it, as we reached the summit, the clouds dispersed and the sun broke through. The speed test was held on the downhill section, which was closed to local traffic, and required an average speed of 31 mph. The roads were wet, and some oil had been discharged by an earlier car, resulting in my car losing traction on a tight, right hand, blind hairpin. I decided, wisely, to glide slowly into the side of the mountain rather than taking the shortest route down, which was over the edge of the road and falling some 5,000 ft to the valley below. Not a difficult decision to make really. Having acquired some very slight damage to the front offside wing, we knew we were not going to make the time set and so, slowly and carefully, we completed the rest of the descent, still utilising the gears and rear drum brakes to slow us down. Despite the accident and our very slow descent, we were surprised that the cars immediately behind us at the summit, did not pass us on the way down.

We arrived at the lunchtime control at Chatillon, within the allocated time, and set about readjusting the front brakes for the afternoon's speed test before having another quick bite to eat. We were able to achieve the set average speed over the Colle Joux immediately after lunch, but the brakes quickly faded again resulting in a slow descent to Verres and our decision to by-pass the afternoon's 120-mile navigational section across Northern Italy.

The final control of the day was some 5 miles away from our hotel that evening, which was located on the shores of Lake Maggiore in the small town of Baveno. During the afternoon, a second very heavy thunderous downpour had resulted in poor visibility and spray. We had not been given the precise location of the final control in the route book, and so we used the tulip diagrams in reverse from the hotel to establish its position. Penalties would have been incurred if we had driven into the control from the wrong direction, so we drove past the marshal with some haste, on the misapprehension that he would not recognise us. We turned round a little further down the road and checked in within our allocated time. The amiable marshal mentioned having seen a car very similar to our own just a few moments earlier, going in the opposite direction, and he asked us to pass on his regards to our twin brothers later that evening, without giving us any penalties. What a decent chap!

When we arrived in the hotel car park, the sun finally broke through the clouds and we noticed that many of the other competing cars had suffered body damage, including four other Austin Healeys, most notable of which was a previously pristine Danish car, which had suffered a head-on collision and was forced to retire. Many other marques suffered similar damage, including a Porsche 356. The front wing and door of the Porsche were almost completely removed, following an altercation with a dislodged large industrial wheelie bin! (That, as they say, is a story for another day.)

After a well-earned sleep, we were up bright and early to fit a new front headlight to our reconfigured front wing and adjust the brakes once more, before setting off soon after 8.30am. The route took us along the northern shores of Lake Maggiore, Lake Lugano and Lake Como, where we experienced some heavy traffic through the main towns. This had some effect on the required average speed set; the organisers clearly had not taken into account the heavily congested roads, but we all continued to make up time wherever possible, dicing with the local traffic. A number of competitors had already been stopped by the local Gendarme in France, and Italy was not going to be any exception. One of our friends in an Austin Healey 3000 was stopped en-route by the Polizia, whilst trying to make up time, and was fined 90 Euros, although I understand that the correct penalty could have been confiscation of their licence, and a team in a Jaguar E-Type was promptly marched off to a local cash machine. Had Dick Turpin been in the Polizia, he would have had a field day!

We arrived at the lunch control in Aprica and immediately set about cleaning and adjusting the brakes for the afternoon speed tests. Today, the speed tests included the notorious Gavia and Stelvio passes. The spectacular Gavia was particularly treacherous, as the road was barely wide enough for one vehicle, let alone two passing each other. However, there were designated passing-points to allow overtaking as we climbed the Gavia. Horns were constantly being used approaching blind bends around the cliff face and whilst overtaking the local traffic. At one particular hairpin, we passed two MGAs which had broken down and, at another further along the pass, a Mini which had blown its engine. A number of cars were also stranded at various points along the Stelvio, including a Volvo Amazon, on which the shoes had completely shattered and the driver was only able to come to a standstill on the very last bend at the bottom of the Stelvio, by slowly running up the grass bank. We also noticed that a Porsche 356 had become stranded due to running out of fuel. On reaching the intermediate control, once we had completed a speed test down the Stelvio, we parked next to an Austin Healey 3000, which had smoke coming from its bonnet. A quick inspection revealed that his disc brakes were on fire.

The Stelvio is the second highest road and pass in Europe, going to a height of 9,000 ft with some 90 hairpins to engage. The downhill descent, which was thankfully closed to normal traffic, was made quite challenging with unmanned roadworks and the regularity section taking place both ways on the same stretch of road. On some of the hairpins, we would encounter another competitor coming in the opposite direction and trying to take the same line. There seemed to be a mutual understanding between the drivers, in these situations, to change lanes and to adopt the English standpoint of driving on the left hand (and correct) side of the road. At the summit, I had been met by a small flock of ducks waddling up the centre of the road, which, although quite captivating and a change from the Alpine cows which we sometimes encountered, was not conducive to our need to keep on the gas. (No ducks were harmed in the completion of this speed test!)

The Stelvio, as previously stated, was tackled in both directions, resulting in two ascents and two descents. By the end of the latter, the brakes were almost completely useless and so our descent was, out of necessity, terribly slow indeed. After completing another downhill speed test at the base of the Stelvio, we were now extremely late and unlikely to make the final control in time. However, the roads through the Vivione to Davos were clear and fast, so we gave it a go, constantly checking the time and remaining distance, whilst we traversed the Ofenpass and Fluela Pass. My petrol gauge was, by now, reading zero with around ten miles to go, and only 12 minutes left to reach the final control. With fingers crossed, we pressed on. Suddenly, with deep banks of snow on either side of the road, the car came to a halt. The spare petrol can was brought out, and we hurriedly refuelled, but sadly missed the control by thirty seconds and were penalised accordingly.

Early the next morning, we set off on the final leg, absolutely shattered, by now, having had no more than 5 hours' sleep each night, and on some, only three hours. After driving around 15 miles from the start we saw a Triumph Spitfire in the middle of the road, hardly recognisable having been involved in a horrific accident. I am not sure what happened, but I am pleased to say that I was later informed that the occupants were able to walk away from the car, which was a complete write-off.

We arrived at the first speed test at Oberalp Pass having maintained the average speed to within 5 seconds of the set time. The next section took us over the notorious Furka Pass, which was, at the time, covered in low cloud. The descent was particularly steep with very tight hairpins, testing my control of the engine speed and use of the rear drum brakes to their limit, bearing in mind I had no front brakes! We were so slow coming down the other side of the pass that once again it was clear, we were not going to reach the lunch control in time. Another detour was considered and adopted, taking us south of the Jungfrau and onto the two final speed tests of the day, thus only missing one long navigational test, which, in any case, was subsequently cancelled due to a road being closed.

Before the first of the afternoon speed tests, we set about removing the front drums and cleaning the remaining fragments of the linings. The linings were right down to the rivets and only allowed the very slightest adjustment. Nevertheless, we were able to achieve particularly good times on the Col des Mosses and Col de la Croix before arriving at the final control of the event, at Villars, bang on our due time!

Of the 105 entries for the Rally, five were non-starters and around 35 cars had to retire due to mechanical failure or accidents. We had achieved our goal of actually finishing the event, despite having no satisfactory brakes for the last five days of the rally. Our overall position was 49th and 11th in Class; not so bad, when you consider that I was nursing the drum brakes for almost the entire rally, whilst most of the cars which finished, had disc brakes and were from the 1960's. If contemplating taking part in the Alpine Rally, with all the ups and, of course, downs, it is certainly preferable to have a car with disc brakes. In the 1954 event, of the 82 cars which left the start, only 40 or so finished. Of the five Austin Healey 100's that took part that year, two retired, one crashed and the remaining cars finished a creditable 25th and 26th overall. We may not have been competitive in the contemporary field, but I can honestly say with some conviction that our participation was as close as it could be to that experienced in the 1954 event.

# TULIP

*Flat out in Holland*

*TULIP*

*Distance: 1,600 miles over 6 days*

*Austin Healey 100M*

First held in 1949, the Tulip is the oldest rally competition in Holland. Whilst in recent years the event has been won almost entirely by Dutch competitors, in the very early days, British entries were quite successful, with Ken Wharton driving Fords and Ian Appleyard driving a Jaguar XK120.

In the 1954 Tulip Rally, 219 competitors left the starting ramp, from seven starting points around Europe, with most British entrants starting from The Hague. Three Austin Healey 100's were entered but achieved no notable success, with one finishing 25th overall, one 128th overall and the other entry crashing. At the time, there was also a speed test at the Zandvoort race circuit, as depicted in the Standard Motor Company film of the period.

Having survived the excitement of the Alpine Rally, my navigator and I decided to tackle the Tulip Rally, which is almost exclusively the home ground of the Dutch rallyist. Learning from our experiences with the Alpine, we carried out further checks in the exhaust department and headed off in our faithful Austin Healey from London to Harwich for the overnight ferry. The ferry operators must have been impressed, as they allowed our car to take pole position on the lower deck, in front of all the lorries, so that we could get away smartly when we docked, rather than being held up on an upper deck with all the hoi polloi in the family saloons and hatchbacks. The crossing was uneventful; the sea was calm and the few long distance lorry drivers amused themselves playing cards. Since we needed to be in Noordwijk shortly after breakfast for scrutineering, it seemed as though the stopwatch was already running before the rally had actually begun!

The Tulip Rally is comparatively kinder on the cars, but the navigation is something else! It probably takes a few years of practice to get yourself into the minds of the organisers and it was evident that the Dutch had a few tricks on the navigation front.

The rally takes place each May, for cars registered in 1968 or earlier, starting on a Monday and finishing five days later on the Saturday. I assume that this is to give those travelling from further afield the chance to get home and freshen up on the Sunday, ready for work on the Monday. The rally uses various map reading systems including, of course, the Tulip Map, with which most rally fans are familiar.

Noordwijk is quite a trendy seaside resort not far from Amsterdam. Each year the rally starts and finishes in Noordwijk's "Huis ter Duin" a large five-star modern hotel. The route normally takes the competitors through Belgium, Luxembourg and France, and on this particular year through Switzerland and Germany too, for good measure. As in the events of the fifties and sixties, the rally travels to the wooded Vosges and the Col de Ballons d'Alsace. Looking at the Michelin map, one sees a number of tight yellow twisty bits on the N465 for some six miles. One tricky hairpin after another. With closed roads, there is a timed ascent, and on the other side of the Col, a timed descent, which is probably more difficult, with its fast sweeping corners and a high average speed set. It was not surprising that no-one overtook anyone else on these sections.

Anyone who knows the Dutch and their love of classic cars, particularly British ones, will also know that they love to party, and throughout the event the bars were always busy until the very early hours, despite the fact that many of the crews were expected to be leaving the starting ramp the next morning at 8am or earlier. With the Dutch marshals despatching the cars at one-minute intervals, I often wonder how many crews were penalised for starting late at the beginning of each day.

As we were in one of the oldest cars in the event, we invariably started early, although, as the rally progressed, we were pushed further back in the starting times. Nevertheless, our early starts didn't stop us joining in with the Dutch at the hotel bars each evening. The Dutch know how to rally hard and play hard, and they also know how to tweak their cars, with all kinds of modifications being allowed. This, to my mind, somehow defeats the object of driving a classic car, but there you go. I personally prefer to experience the cars as they left the factory, as their maker intended, warts and all.

It was evident, on arrival, that many of the participants had taken part for several years previously with drivers and navigators alike proudly displaying their annual lapel badges held on a link bar for all to see. There were only five British teams in a field of just over 200 cars taking part. Still, with a Dutch name like "van Maanen" we were clearly not going to be out of place, in this company. We were informed that the route was going to be the longest that had been devised for many years; they must have known we were coming. The other British Teams included an ex-Works TR2 from 1954, a 1960 Austin Healey 3000, a 1965 Lotus Cortina and a 1962 TR4. On the starting ramp each entrant would be introduced to the large crowd gathered, with the local TV station broadcasting the event nationwide, such is the popularity of the Tulip.

We arrived at the "Huis ter Duin" or Hotel of the Dunes, in Noordwijk and were made most welcome by all the other entrants; my knowledge of the Dutch language is quite limited, so it was a good thing that the Dutch speak such good English. Being the third oldest car participating in the Sporting Class, we were fortunate that there were two other later Austin Healey 100M's to keep us company. One of the 100M's was a father and son team, Pieter and Jeroen Booij, the latter being a motoring journalist, who would become particularly good friends for many years to come. Indeed, I took part in a few more competitive rallies with Jeroen including the Classic Gelderlandrit in Southern Holland, which was a real blast.

The navigation on the Tulip Rally is fiendish in the extreme, with numerous tricks to catch out the uninformed, including hidden letter boards, used to check that you are not cutting out sections between the speed tests. In addition, it seemed that every village in Belgium and Holland has speed humps over deeply rutted cobbled streets, which was not favourable for low-slung Healeys.

We were off to a good start when, to our annoyance, whilst taking a sharp right-hand bend during the morning stage, a tyre blew. A quick tyre change, and then off to the nearest tyre repair garage at lunchtime. Whilst we, of course, had a spare tyre, it was thought prudent to take advantage of the tyre repair shop as we were passing, just in case lightning was to strike twice in a more remote location. In the 1950's, a penalty was imposed for changing the brand of the tyres used, and so it was important to preserve your tyres. It was a great shame as we were doing so well, with no wrong slots on the route, but I suppose that is one of the "joys" of rallying.

Holland, or the Netherlands, is a low lying country, so the scenery was not particularly awe inspiring; indeed each road looked very much like the one before, as we traced around the various fields laid out in large rectangles. We were, by now, heading for Northern France and eventually on to the main control for the event, at Hotel Le Lac at Malbuisson which would become our base for the next two days whilst we travelled through the Jura Mountains and the Col de La Faucille.

On one stage the following day, which was along the dirt tracks of the dense Forest Plantation in the Vosges Mountains, an MGA in front of us had taken

the wrong turning and ended up stuck in deep mud, which came up above the wheel arches. We tried to help get him out, but to no avail. A Samaritan in the guise of a Volvo Amazon went to help, but it became stuck too! The rally recovery truck was called for, but even this vehicle struggled in the seriously deep mud. This experience made us take a little more caution whenever we came to a junction in the forest, just in case we took the wrong route and ended up in a similar predicament. With all the dust and dirt we encountered on the forest sections, the carburettors started coughing a little, which meant we had to stop to clean out the feed pipes and adjust them, but we still managed to make it to the controls without penalty.
After the Vosges Mountains we continued on to the Ballon d'Alsace, a well known hill climb, where we encountered some well surfaced, fast sweeping road sections, closed to local traffic, allowing the competitors to really have a blast, which was a great laugh.

Despite some navigational confusion, such as mistaking a narrow farm track for a huge dual carriageway, we were doing rather well, keeping on the correct route and not gaining too many penalties. It clearly pays to remain calm on such competitive events and for the driver and navigator to give each other some slack. Indeed, it is during times like this that friendships are made and lost.

Unlike the Alpine, this time the exhaust did stay on, although we needed to stop a couple of times to check the brackets, as we ventured along some extremely poor unmade roads. The suspension on many of the cars took a hammering, resulting in some major rebuilds to suspension mounts at the final control each day, particularly after the lengthy forest section in the Vosges Mountains. We noticed that a Mercedes Gullwing appeared to be having its entire rear axle replaced outside the Hotel Le Lac at Malbuisson. This Mercedes was actually part of a Museum exhibition in Holland, so it was great to see this automotive work of art being used as it was intended. As ever, towards the end of our stay in the Jura, the car park at the end of the day, with its damaged or missing wings, doors, radiators, broken half shafts etc., it was more akin to a second hand car lot!

With France behind us, the roads became straighter and the countryside flatter, we left Luxembourg to re-enter the Netherlands for the long drag back to Noordwijk. On some of the sections, out on the flat open road with good visibility and no traffic whatsoever, we were flat out keeping up with the likes of the Works TR2 and a collection of 1960's rally-prepared vehicles. It was great fun, as, with their enthusiasm, you would occasionally see one of them disappear down a road in front of you, which was not on the route and then a short while later you would see them in your rear mirror trying to blast pass you again.

Once we were back in Holland, rather than using a Tulip Map, the organisers had arranged a passage through a large town, which was in a grid format. Essentially, we had to follow the grid pattern very carefully to ensure we kept on the correct route, which is no mean feat when the Dutch houses all looked very similar and there were no standout landmarks to assist with the navigation.

Having completed a few fast sections, we visited the DAF Trucks testing ground and the Philips Factory at Eindhoven for some speed tests, no doubt to replace the five lap races at the Zandvoort circuit, which was originally part of the event in the early 1950's. The pace was beginning to hot up and the navigation was becoming harder now that we were in sight of the finish. A dozen or so cars broke down during the speed tests, so it was with some relief that we were able to limp home. Thankfully, our brakes also held out, although they had been seriously tested in the Jura Mountains.

At the finish in Noordwijk, a couple of young Dutch girls, in traditional costume, showered a large bouquet of tulips over each of the cars as we finally made it onto the Finishers ramp. There were huge crowds and television cameras at the finish to welcome the cars back. So important was it to finish, that some competitors, who had broken down on the last day, possibly during the speed tests, resorted to trailering their cars to within sight of the Finish, so that they could try to drive the last mile or so and take part in all the excitement.

The hotel car park was a sight to behold with cars covered in mud, with bent fenders, missing lights and other non-factory regalia, which indicated that no-one had held back. The owners of the cars were clearly people not that interested in concours events!

The prize-giving reception within the Grand "Huis ter Duin" was a splendid affair, being a black tie do with a wonderful spread of food and live bands playing jazz and swing into the early hours. The reception was held in the Ballroom, located on the second floor of the Hotel, which was reached via a magnificent wide double staircase. Those teams which had won their class received a beautiful Silver Tulip trophy for their efforts, which were the same as those awarded in the original event. As we waited to hear the overall winner of the event, suddenly, without any prior warning, the lights were switched off, the two large entrance doors to the ballroom flung open (you will recall that we are on the second floor) and there, with the engine at full revs and headlights ablaze was the winning Volvo 122 entering the room on the red carpet. It was quite a spectacular entrance! The driver and navigator were perched on top of the roof of the Volvo spraying champagne over themselves and anyone unfortunate, or maybe fortunate, to be within range. As we were sitting right by the red carpet, we didn't need a top up from the wine waiters! Just in case you were wondering, a car lift had been installed at the Huis ter Duin by a local Ferrari Dealership, when the Hotel was built.

Waking up, bleary-eyed, early on Sunday, the day of our return home, we spent a few hours walking along the promenade and on the pebble beach to get some fresh sea air and to relax after the gruelling days on the rally, before returning to the hotel, packing and saying our farewells.

Once again despite adversity, we had achieved our goal by finishing the rally, although we ended up halfway down the field. We actually came 11th out of 18 in our Pre-1960 Class, which was really not so bad.

This rally is very well organised and offers a true reflection of the Tulip Rally of the 1950's and 1960's. Indeed, several famous rally drivers from that period, including Dries Jetten, regularly take part. It's a great shame that more teams from outside Holland do not enter, particularly as it is so easily reached from the UK and takes in some great roads in the Jura Mountains. One word of warning though, as mentioned, when entering Holland there are many speed humps to negotiate, so make sure your suspension and exhaust is up to the task.

# LIEGE

*In the footsteps of Hannibal*

*LIEGE*

*Distance: 1,600 miles in 5 days*

*Austin Healey 100M*

We often hear that all roads lead to Rome. Well, for this event, that statement is true, except that when the event was is in its heyday, the rally took the competitors from Liege to Rome and back to Liege. The Liege, nicknamed "The Road Marathon", has taken place since 1931, with 18 events up until 1960, primarily for GT cars, which is when it was stopped, having been recognised by the organisers as the hardest and fastest of rallies in its day. Indeed, the Liege was timed to an impossible schedule, which intensified when the rally moved to Yugoslavia and Bulgaria in the early 1960's. The last Liege Rome Liege, which took place in 1960, was won by Pat Moss and Ann Wisdom in an Austin Healey 3000. In that year, of the many entrants taking part, only thirteen cars finished the event out of around 100 starters.

Thankfully, the current adaptation is not quite so demanding and is an "invitation only" event with no post-1960 cars. There were just over 100 entrants, to match that of the original event in the 1950's, along with our Austin Healey, which made for quite an impressive line-up. One was reminded of the undertaking set by Hannibal in crossing the Alps into Italy some 1800 years earlier. We were hopeful that our adventure would be just as epic.

The cars gathered in the cobbled central courtyard of the magnificent Palais des Princes Eveques, in the city centre of Liege, with the Mayor and other dignitaries in attendance, to flag the cars off at the start. The rally was greatly oversubscribed, with a final total of 103 cars actually taking the flag. The year before saw over 200 starters, but this was considered to be far too many by both the organisers and the competitors. After being flagged off, the route would take the field through the Black Forest, the Alps and finally, via Tuscany, to Rome, with temperatures each day being well over 30C. Inevitably, the cars and their occupants would suffer from the heat.

The Liege differs from most other rallies in its attempt to get back to the original format and the spirit of the original event, by only allowing a few certain modifications. This means that the navigators are not allowed any Haldas or Trip meters and must rely only on the car's trip. The navigation, however, was reasonably straight forward once we had got used to the smallest incremental reading from the odometer, being 1/10th of a mile, and had calculated the error factor of the read out to the true, which in our case was a remarkable 0.8%. One of the vintage Bentleys taking part was 12% from true!

The organisers of the Liege had an ingenious electronic chip on the timecard, to check that all the vehicles were always following the planned route and maintaining appropriate speeds.

My companion for the Liege was a very experienced navigator, with various round-the-world, and cross-continent, trips under his belt. Bizarrely, he seems to get great enjoyment out of making calculations and reading maps and charts, whilst being thrown around in the passenger seat. Our first hotel, where scrutineering and a drivers' briefing took place, was the Post Hotel, which stands high up in the hills overlooking the city of Liege; this allowed us time for an early check over after our two hour drive from the channel ferry port at Calais.

After an early start from Liege on the Saturday morning, we drove through undulating forest scenery, across Luxembourg, and on to Baden-Baden in Germany for the first night stop. Despite the relatively easy navigation, we managed to wrong-slot early on, and unfortunately this came at the worst possible moment on day one, just prior to three successive regularity checks, which cost us quite a few points. Nevertheless, the route chosen was splendid, with some fabulous scenery over undulating hills through the Black Forest; some locations being reminiscent of the Sound of Music. I do believe that I heard Miss Andrews at one point, exclaiming that the hills were alive.

On arrival in Baden-Baden, we were met by some delightful young ladies in local costume, who delivered a flute of champagne to each of us, accompanied by a peck on the cheek. Now that's what I call a welcome! We had started to notice strong petrol smells as the day wore on which, we discovered, was due to a leak from the front carburettor. A bit of tinkering each day seemed to do the trick.

The second day saw us driving across the Swiss Alps, with trials on several of the famous passes, principally the St Gothard. The speed test on the St Gothard Pass included a downhill timed section, where we needed to maintain an average speed of 30mph, whilst tackling 15 or so hairpins on a slightly damp cobbled road. We set off at pace to reach the necessary average speed, but maintaining that speed for the entire section proved to be too much for our car's puny brake shoes. It was at this point that we started to suffer severe brake fade which, unfortunately, would persist throughout the rally. Shortly after the Gothard, we noticed that the car temperature was soaring to boiling point, which turned out to be due to a shredded fan belt. A new one was effortlessly fitted by us at the roadside, in the heat of the day, and then we were off again to experience some frustrating navigation problems immediately ahead of our lunch break in Zurich; this was due to all city centre roads being closed for a local Marathon running event of the tatty trainer type. Zurich couldn't cope with two marathons on the same day! In common with several other competitors, it took us a full hour to weave our way through the outskirts to the lunch halt, arriving just in time to sign in and immediately sign out again, so no lunch for many of us that day. We fared better in the afternoon and arrived on time for the final control and the night's sojourn in Stresa, the hotel being charmingly situated on the shore of Lake Maggiore.

Day three saw the competition intensify, with several tight Regularity and Hill Climb sections, which we successfully completed, as we drove ever southward in the blazing sun to reach the Mediterranean coast at Rapallo that evening. For the final miles along a ravine into Rapallo, we followed a 1954 Bentley R-Type Continental, which was being driven with some gusto by Christian Hueber, who co-wrote a splendid book on this model, and we were accompanied by Italian Police motorbike out-riders, who followed us right into the town centre. Townspeople with small children were sitting on walls and roof tops to get a good vantage point, to see the cars as we meandered along. On arrival in Rapallo, the cars gathered at a small petrol station in the city centre and caused quite a stir, with all the interest and police support. We finally made it to the underground car park of the Excelsior Palace Hotel, which overlooks the Portofino coastline. I then spent an enjoyable hour or so helping Christian Hueber, who was sporting his Plus Fours, and meticulously carrying out his daily checks on his Bentley, which was parked right alongside our Austin Healey, before we headed in for supper and a well-earned rest. It later transpired that an Austin Healey 100S, on its first major outing for many years, suffered damage to the sump, causing all the engine oil to be discharged over the road, near the city centre petrol station. Somehow, the car limped to a local garage, which was open all night, the sump was repaired and the 100S was able to resume the rally the following day.

Tuesday was the penultimate day, during which the rally utilised some spectacular scenic inland routes through this part of Tuscany, which we were able to enjoy without any dramas, whilst driving to our overnight stop at Grosseto. Having suffered temperatures in excess of 40C, my navigator was not in the mood to wait a couple of hours for the main course of our evening meal. To the amusement of our table, with the waiters not able to cope with the surge in diners arriving at the same time, my navigator took matters into his own hands and stormed into the kitchen, knife and fork in hand, to have "a word" with the chef. It came as no surprise that our table was served a few minutes later.

After supper, whilst my navigator took a rest in the bedroom to calm down, in the early evening light, I spent some time adjusting the brakes and checking the shoe linings, which were suffering once again. On noticing the poor state of the linings, I wondered if I should risk carrying on and possibly damaging the original drums, so I sought advice from the illustrious Alastair Caldwell, whose AC Aceca was parking next to our Austin Healey. Alastair, who was previously the Formula One Team manager for McLaren throughout the 1970s and a regular participant in historic rallies around the world, reminded me of the cost of taking part in this event which put things into perspective, regarding the cost of skimming the drums when I returned home. I decided to go for it. No doubt Alastair had made similar decisions at McLaren to achieve their success in the Formula One World Championships.

Our final run, the next day, took us around the shores of the expansive Lake Bolsena and further southwards towards a holding point in the northern suburbs of Rome, where we were due to arrive by lunchtime. During the morning stages, we had made an impromptu stop for water, an espresso and, of course, some local gelato. As we re-joined the main road, we tucked in behind a vintage Talbot, which was leading the event, and were able to enjoy an exclusive escort by the Italian Polizia Stradale, for about 50 miles or so, through villages and towns, ignoring the traffic lights and road signals, as all non-rally traffic had been stopped so that we could make good progress to the holding point outside Rome.

At the holding point we met up with no fewer than 24 police motorcyclists and half a dozen police cars and were told by an experienced hand from previous Liege rallies that the best was yet to come. How right he was! As soon as a dozen rally cars had gathered, the whistles and sirens started in a crescendo of noise and, with little time to think, off we went, driving in convoy at speeds in excess of 60 mph, right through the heart of a congested Rome at Peak Rush Hour. We had been told by the police to follow the riders closely and not to back off the gas. The truly skilful Italian Police Motorbike riders ensured that all other traffic was halted and moved out of the way, as we went through red lights and down one-way streets the wrong way. It was an amazing and exhilarating experience. We marvelled at the police motorcyclists standing proud of their saddles on occasion, turning round to wave a stop signal at the other traffic, and all the time steering their machines, with the other hand. All this at breakneck speed with whistles and sirens blaring constantly. Despite all the chaos, the locals all seemed to enjoy the convoy of classic cars, and many local motorists simply got out of their cars to find out what was causing the commotion and to watch the spectacle.

And so the rally finished on a zenith in the Parc Ferme in Villa Borghese overlooking central Rome, where the cars could shelter under the trees and spectators were able to look around the cars. At last, it was time to relax and reflect. We were staying at the splendid Westin Excelsior Hotel, where we were able to enjoy a few hours relaxing in the spa, with temperatures outside being higher than in the hotel's sauna!

Clearly this retrospective rally is no way near as arduous as the original event, with most, if not all, the starters making it to the finish. The greatest challenge on the year we took part, seemed to be the outside temperatures, so if you are thinking about taking part, make sure you have plenty of water on board. The rally was well organised and great fun, with the final run into Rome being exhilarating and an experience not to be missed. We achieved 7th in class, which was an exceptionally good result in such a strong field and had we not made a wrong slot at the beginning of the rally, we might have brought away some silverware. The final black tie dinner was quite a splendid affair at a nearby hotel, which was not as grand as other rallies we had been on, but nevertheless, it was a good opportunity to catch up with our fellow competitors and to say our farewells.

As a postscript, having made it to the finish, the adventure continued. We had originally planned to drive back to the Calais ferry, stopping off at a couple of hotels in Northern Italy and France along the way, but with the ridiculously high temperatures, as we drove out of Rome, we wondered if there might be an alternative way back. You may remember the British Rail advertising slogan from the 1980's "Let the train take the strain". We did, and decided to see if we could make the motorail service from Nice in Southern France to Hertogenbosch in Holland. Luckily, my navigator, who banks with Coutts &

Co in London, was able to speak with his personal assistant at the bank, who arranged some tickets for the motorail, while we continued driving up the motorway. Not sure you would get that kind of service from any High Street branch. The journey from Rome to Nice is around 400 miles, so we needed to have a clear run on the motorways and thankfully that was the case. We made the dash to Nice Central Railway Station with just minutes to spare; it felt like we were back on the rally. Once on the train, we were able to sit back to enjoy a leisurely overnight trip back to Holland in the comfort of two bunk beds, before an uneventful drive home the following day, with no further time penalties to worry about, save making it indoors in time for tea.

# YPRES

*Orchestral Maneouvres in the Dark*

*YPRES*

*Distance: 450 miles over 3 days*

*Austin Healey 100M*

As a slight diversion from the major events I had normally taken part in, I felt it was worth attempting the Ypres Retro Rally organised by the AC Targa Florio and Three Castles MC. There were a number of smaller rallies which attracted the amateurs in the early 1950's, such as Lyons-Charbonnières, Rheinlandfahrt and Paris – St Raphael. The Austin Healey 100 achieved some great results in these events, including first in class and we made it our mission to do likewise. In my opinion, this is the kind of rally which is so reminiscent of those competitions which were commonplace in the immediate post-war period, and which were not so attractive to the main factory works teams and therefore was the domain of the amateur. Nevertheless, these early events still had a combination of regularities, timed sections and special tests to give the amateurs a flavour of competition.

It was a pleasant surprise to find that the rally was to have a base hotel for the duration of the event, which would have significant advantages. Apart from solving the logistics of having to transport all your attire, including dinner jackets, there was also the benefit of filling up with petrol at a familiar petrol station each evening in readiness for the following day. The rally organisers required the cars to be as near their original specification as possible, with no provision for rally specs. One other particular feature, which also attracted the amateur entrants, was the lengthy night stage.

The event started gently enough, with scrutineering on the Friday being conveniently located in the hotel underground car park. There was plenty of camaraderie as everyone got to know their fellow competitors, whilst borrowing various items required to meet the organisers' demands, such as tow ropes, groundsheets and so on. All this killed some time as we waited for the rally to start that afternoon in the nearby village of Boezinge, utilising the ramp used to start the notorious 24-hour Championship Rally. The first section involved driving around the labyrinth of narrow country lanes in the flat, nondescript Flanders area. Following this, was a speed trial, a single speed regularity by tulips, followed by another based on map reading. The organisers had given us a taster of what was to come, as this was clearly going to be a tough rally, and there was a gradual, but persistent, increase in pace as the event unfolded. Our initial attempts at the driving speed test along a two-mile closed road section, around cones, caused some merriment for the watching marshals, who described our efforts as the "Laurel and Hardy" approach. Once we had devised a method of deciding if "left" meant keep left of the cone or whether the cone should be to the left, we quickly got the hang of things and picked up some good times.

Saturday, as anticipated, was the real challenge, with an exceedingly long and uncompromising session. The first car left at 8.30am and, although a break was given at lunchtime and again for supper at 7pm, the pressure was relentless, until we finally rolled into the hotel car park, exhausted, at 3am the following morning. During the early evening, the rain cleared and beams were adjusted for the night section. We had been apprehensive about the night section, and particularly when we learnt only an hour before the "off", that the section was to navigate from maps only with no tulips, and we were handed two A3 sized colour maps, depicting no fewer than 77 passage and time controls to visit, signified by small dots on the map which looked as though it had contracted chicken pox. The organisers had used every trick in the book to ensure that it wasn't easy. The instructions had three variable speed regularities, timed to the second, during the night run. The organisers had clearly decided to cause chaos, bearing in mind that we were driving much of the route in complete darkness, with no streetlights and in remote locations.

We found the night section difficult to begin with, having wrong-slotted a couple of times early on, and much to the annoyance of my navigator who was beginning to feel a little queasy being tossed around on the single track road at night, we did not stop to get the Rennies located in the boot, so that we didn't lose any time. However, we correctly, in hindsight, ditched any attempt at simultaneously checking regularity speeds, and concentrated on simply staying on the correct course, especially as it was obvious that the times given were pretty tight. After a shaky start we got better and better and developed a technique which worked very well. In fact, despite deliberately missing out one passage control because the highlighted potholed road leading to the control may have irretrievably damaged our low slung exhaust, this stage proved to be the highlight of the rally for us, and ultimately the most rewarding when we discovered in the morning, that despite our dismissal of time checks, we had improved our ranking from 8th to 4th overall!

We had had some interesting moments at junctions, including one crossroads, where four competitors approached it from all four directions. Someone must have been right, but who? One of the rally teams comprised a group of RAF Engineers driving a couple of Hillman Imps; it was great fun watching them overtake us at breakneck speed, only to see them coming back at a similar velocity and passing us in the opposite direction 10 minutes later. Clearly, they had some difficulty map reading. In view of the intense concentration required whilst driving at night, when we arrived at the Rally HQ Hotel Flanders Fields, in the early hours, we decided that it would be a great idea to get a quick shot of whisky before retiring to calm the nerves. The streets around the Hotel were eerily silent and deserted, but, across the street from the Hotel, was a very small pub with what appeared to be a slight glow from within. Intrigued, we approached the front door and gingerly opened it. To our amazement, we were confronted by the deafening roar of virtually every rally crew in the event, having a few beers and discussing anecdotes arising from the problems of chasing each other along farm tracks, around the consistently bland, flat countryside at night. The pub was packed, and a jolly good time was had by all.

Essentially, we had all been following a couple of small bright red taillights in the distance, although in our case, the car following us was attracted to

the sparks coming from our low exhaust on the rough tracks. You may have noted within this book, that I have generally refrained from mentioning the names of navigators or fellow competitors, for fear of any repercussions, which may result in them refusing to buy me a beer at the bar, but I believe a few characters are worth mentioning, such as the amiable but mischievous Robert Coucher, who is the well-known, long serving International Editor of the hugely successful Octane magazine, which had been launched the year prior to us taking part in this event. It was Robert who had been following us that night in his fabulous 1300cc Lancia Fulvia, and to this day, we have remained good friends and he still refers to me, many years later, as "Sparks". It had been a thoroughly enjoyable evening and night, with the entrants all giving their cars some stick, which we enjoyed immensely. Headlights danced around the fields in various directions, with horns blaring constantly like a symphony of chaos.

The final day of the rally was no less competitive, with numerous tight regularities still to come before the final flag was dropped at the civilised time of 5pm, in time to dress up for the traditional black-tie dinner. Unfortunately, we suffered our one and only mechanical problem in the morning, just ahead of a time control, when the engine died and an investigation proved that the fuel line clip had sheared, resulting in petrol gushing onto the road below. It took me around 15 minutes to clean it out and fix, as we didn't have a suitably sized replacement clip; however, with a bit of ingenuity and a smidgen of luck, we managed to get back on the road again. The delay had cost us maximum penalty points at the next control, but most importantly we were still in the running. The support crew for the rally supplied the necessary replacement part at our lunchtime break, giving us a more permanent repair so that we could confidently finish the rally.

There was a battle for the top place overall between a bright orange Ford Anglia putting in a superb performance to just pip an MGB. Of the 48 cars entered for the event, we managed to finish 6th overall and first in class for pre-1959 cars, achieving our goal of replicating the success of those amateur drivers with their Austin Healey 100's in period.

Prior to the final gala dinner, we attended the brief memorial ceremony, which has been held every evening since 1928, under the impressive archway of the "Menin Gate". The Gate is inscribed with the names of 58,000 soldiers who had lost their lives in The Great War, but were never found. The memorial was attended that evening by a thousand or so onlookers, which I understand is quite typical. The "last post" was sounded by three buglers with not a murmur from the crowd. In recognition of having won our class, my navigator and I were honoured to be asked by the local Mayor and dignitaries, to lay a wreath on behalf of the Ypres Rally, as an act of remembrance for the 250,000 English and Commonwealth soldiers who had lost their lives in the nearby battlefields. After this brief but very moving episode, we attended the final Black-Tie dinner in the splendidly atmospheric 15th Century Cloth Hall and took time to reflect on the event.

The Ypres Rally was one of the most professionally organised rallies, with Interim Results swiftly prepared and made available after each major section. The marshalling was exemplary with no cutting back of officials or course marshals. There have been rallies where, after following numerous long loops and losing time, and not coming across a single marshal, there was a real temptation to cut further long winding segments in order to make up time and still be assured that no penalty would be incurred. Not on this rally though, with marshals everywhere to keep the competitors on their toes. There wasn't a single error in the road books, which again is quite unusual, especially on the night section, which must have taken a considerable amount of preparation. It was refreshing to have such accuracy, professionalism and congeniality in the rally organisers. A great event for all levels of experience.

*Taking a solo run up the Stelvio – Alpine*

*Teams sharing experiences, whilst at a Passage Control in Malbuisson – Tulip*

*St Gottard Pass Control – Liege*

*Preparing for police escort on the outskirts of Rome – Liege*

*Piazza Grande in Arezzo – Cento Ore*

*Passage Control near San Lorenzo – Picos Pyrennes*

*Making the finishing ramp in Brescia – Mille Miglia*

*Getting ready for a Hill Climb near Agrigento – Targa Florio*

# MILLE MIGLIA

*The Tifosi Tour*

MILLE MIGLIA

Distance: 1,000 miles over 3 days

Ferrari 330GT

The Donald Healey Motor Company had some notable success in the Mille Miglia in the late 1940's with Warwick-built Healeys being the only British cars to take part in the event. In 1953 two Austin Healey 100's took part in the race but both retired, and in 1954, of the three Austin Healey 100S's which entered, two retired. The remaining one was brought home by Lance Macklin; it had finished 23rd overall, 5th in class and was the first British car to receive the Mille Miglia's chequered flag. Having driven the race on his own without a co-driver, Lance Macklin apparently likened the event to a one-lap Grand Prix of interminable length, but more interesting than covering lap after lap of the same circuit. Clearly, to finish the race, which was on public roads, was not as straight forward as you might think. Indeed, there were a couple of fatal accidents in 1954. In 1955, two Austin Healey 100S's took part, driven by George Abecassis and Lance Macklin, finishing 11th and 36th respectively, and one solitary standard Austin Healey 100, which finished 88th overall and 4th in class, and was driven by a Mr Ferrari.

As has been well recorded, Stirling Moss, with the assistance of Denis Jenkinson, and his notorious roller scroll, or more affectionately known as "The Bog Roll" for pace notes, achieved a record time in 1955 of 10 hours and 7 minutes, which remains unbeaten, in a Mercedes Benz 300SLR. I have met up with Sir Stirling Moss and Lady Susie Moss at various events over the years, and I remember being seated next to them one afternoon, at a small bar in Saint Leonard des Bois in France, watching a Grand Prix and being blown away by the encyclopaedic knowledge of Lady Susie Moss on Formula

One. I have often wondered if her wisdom might also extend to the Mille Miglia, but, unfortunately, never got round to asking her.

I had a dilemma. With the limited success of the standard Austin Healey 100 in the Mille Miglia and one of the few finishers having a Mr Ferrari at the wheel, it seemed inevitable that I would finally decide to honour the Tifosi and chose a Ferrari to compete in the modern day historic race. As they say, "When in Rome...".

There are some 1500-2000 applicants for around 360 places in the Historic Mille Miglia race, coming from all corners of the world, but you need to have a car of special interest; perhaps one that competed in the event in period or one which would have been driven by a famous racing driver. A number of ex-Formula One drivers take part each year with factory and museum entries. As only relatively few Ferraris took part in period, and only a handful take part in the retrospective historic event, and with the home crowds wanting more of their national cars taking part, the Ferrari Factory created a Mille Miglia Tribute, in which old Ferraris manufactured after 1957 could take part. This Tribute allows a further 100 cars to take part in the event. The Historic Mille Miglia and the Ferrari Tribute travel along the same route, use the same road book, undertake the same time trials, check points etc, and so the two events are essentially the same. The best part though, is that the Tribute starts a couple of hours before the Historic and so if you have an old Ferrari, you are effectively leading the entire event. Our 1966 Ferrari 330GT, which had disc brakes, was the eighth oldest car in the Tribute, so the pressure was on.

When taking part in such events further afield, it is my opinion that it is not only cost effective, when one considers fuel, hotels, ferries, tolls etc, but also easier on the car, to simply have it transported to the event, fly out to join the rally and be re-united with your vehicle at the start. There are a few specialist transportation companies who offer this service, with containers that will each comfortably take some 6 cars, helping to reduce costs for the individual. My car was loaded in London, along with a few other entrants' cars for transportation to Brescia.

With all local schools and offices closing for the event, there is a carnival atmosphere and apparently, aside from the TV audiences, more than 4 million people line the route from start to finish. It is a fantastic feeling to be cheered on by such a noisy and enthusiastic crowd. This event certainly has the "wow" factor, and has been sponsored for many years by Chopard, a high-end Swiss watchmaker, who produce a special edition Mille Miglia chronograph watch every year for those taking part. These watches are beautifully presented and provide a wonderful keepsake for the competitors, should they choose to purchase one.

Within the Historic Mille Miglia there are always some amazing cars, including numerous Bugatti Type 37's, Ferrari 340's, at least a dozen Mercedes Gullwings, pre-war Mercedes SSK's and beautiful Bentley Blowers. I have owned a 1930 Bentley Open Tourer for many years, using her to take part in rallies around Europe, but I stand in awe of those drivers who use their vintage cars to take part in the more competitive rally events mentioned in this book. Trying to negotiate hairpins at speed is not for the fainthearted and attempting to skirt around local traffic on busy roads is no mean feat. No doubt driving such vintage cars in longer rallies, perhaps through Outer Mongolia on the Peking to Paris, has its own dramas, but to me driving a vintage car in these retrospective, competitive rallies is astonishing.

Having been inspected by a senior engineer from Maranello in the UK, our Ferrari was taken by the transporter to a large industrial unit on the outskirts of Brescia, which was being used for scrutineering. It was wonderful to see all the competitors' cars together. It was quite a long process, placing all the various sponsorship stickers onto the car, having the transponders fixed, so that the organisers can get a GPS fixing for the cars along the route, and, of course, receiving the timing cards and route books.

After further scrutineering, we travelled a short distance to the town centre and tried to find a parking spot to take in the atmosphere with all the 420 other cars, which had entered the race. There were large crowds in the town centre, with people vying for positions to see the cars slowly progressing through further checks, before taking their place at the start. It seemed like organised chaos. We slowly crept to the start line in the Piazza della Loggia in the centre of Brescia and were flagged off, but before we had even reached Padova, one of the two mechanical fuel pumps on the car failed. We rerouted the fuel lines to by-pass the faulty pump and got going again, using a secondary electric pump, as a back-up, which expired each time we were going flat out up a hill, which was often!

The run down to Ravenna late in the evening and into the early hours was magical. Hearing the V12 engine at full chat, with the noise bouncing off the walls of the terraced houses, through some small villages, which had closed road sections and huge grandstands full of excited spectators, was amazing. The local police were waving at us to go faster, calling out "Avanti, Avanti!", much to the amusement of those standing close by. At each corner there were dozens of camera flashes going off, which did sometimes dazzle us, but the roar of the crowds was something never to be forgotten.

We eventually arrived in Ravenna at around 2am and headed straight to the hotel for a mere three hours' sleep, before waking up and setting off again for the Principality of San Marino and on to Rome. The long climb up to the San Risparmio in the centre of San Marino with all the local traffic wasn't great but we eventually got through, with several cars overheating. After clearing San Marino, the roads opened up towards Sansepolcro, where we drove into the town square, with the car running beautifully, and with the one fuel pump working. We were making good progress.

As we approached Rome, we were meticulously split into groups and escorted through the crowded streets by Italian police motorbikes, blue lights flashing, stopping the traffic and guiding us down one-way streets the wrong way, all at a lively pace. Locals stuck in traffic were sometimes reluctant to give way to the newcomers, until a policeman on a motorbike gave them a gentle gesture with his boot! Terrific stuff. In the centre of Rome, the participants on the

Tribute were individually presented to Luca Di Montezemolo, who was the Ferrari President at the time, before we completed a lap of all the major landmarks, with huge crowds waving and cheering, and cameras flashing.

We parked in an underground car park in the centre of Rome overnight and grabbed another three hours sleep at some five-star hotel. No doubt you will have gathered that sleep time was at a premium, so the rating of the hotel wasn't that important. Indeed, many of the entrants took time during the night to undertake some checks and repairs before the following day and so they decided to simply take a nap in their cars! The next morning, we woke early at around 4am to get back to the garage in order to prepare the car for the trip to the Vallelunga circuit for some speed tests, and then onto Viterbo. This section of the rally between Radiocofani and Buonconvento, can only be described as the best part of the route, with stunning fast sweeping left and right bends over the undulating hills.

Eventually we entered the historic city of Siena, and having negotiated the crowds in the Piazza del Campo, where the famous Palio horserace takes place each year, we were directed up one of the very narrow and steep cobbled streets up out of the Piazza, and to our dismay the second mechanical fuel pump expired!! If we were to breakdown in such a narrow street, being at the front of the race, we could potentially stop the entire event, so I carefully pulled the car to one side, as close as possible to the shop fronts, so that the rest of the field could squeeze past. It meant my stopping the car immediately across a shop doorway. I jumped out of the car and slid underneath to see if I could knock the remaining mechanical fuel pump back into action, at which point a very angry looking shop owner came out waving his hands in the air with alarm. He was clearly concerned that I might be preventing tourists from entering his shop. My response was to politely ask him if he would kindly pass me a wrench to knock the fuel pump. It was a bit of a risk, but thankfully, he didn't use the wrench on me! Anyway, I managed to quickly get the fuel pump working again and being that we were on a very steep slope, the car pulled away slowly.

Having left Siena, we motored on to San Casciano Val Di Pesa; a small mountain village for a brief respite, a sandwich and glass of wine (we were drinking gallons of bottled water during the event, which could only satisfy us to a certain extent), and then we were off to Florence. It was fun driving through the large crowds which had gathered to see the race pass by around the Ponte Vecchio, where the spectators were up to six people deep. It is not always possible to use the road book in the City centres, so you simply follow the crowds and the car in front! The support teams and cars accompanying the entrants are not allowed to enter the City centres with the race cars, so the event traffic is kept to the bare minimum.

Our back-up electric fuel pump was now overheating, so we needed to let it cool down whenever we stopped at check points. The drive back to Brescia via the Futa Pass, Bologna and Modena, where a further speed test on the official Ferrari Test Track at Maranello was included, was exhilarating. It was getting towards dusk, the light was fading, and a few locals, with their modern Ferraris and Lamborghinis, started joining in and dicing with the competitors. Whilst these individuals might have felt that overtaking several race cars at a time would be an exciting experience, it was also extremely dangerous and stupid, but thankfully there were no mishaps to our knowledge. Anyway, with one temperamental mechanical fuel pump working, we finally reached Brescia late in the evening and queued up to drive onto the finishing ramp around midnight to receive the chequered flag.

There is a Shell film of the 1953 edition directed by Bill Mason, which is well worth a look. At the end of the film a new proverb is given in honour of Clemente Biondetti, "The King of the Mille Miglia", who had won the race no fewer than four times. With his co-driver, he had pushed his Lancia Aurelia B20 over two miles, uphill, to cross the finishing line, which was an amazing feat after driving non-stop for almost 12 hours. The proverb is "The heart is more important than the engine". How true is that.

I am not sure where we finished or how many cars completed the race, save that there were several cars which had broken down along the way. With there being many support vehicles, I would imagine that several of the cars had a very good supply of spare parts to ensure that they completed the route. We had been blessed with good weather throughout and enjoyed some amazing roads. I haven't been a spectator at the Mille Miglia, but from what we could see whilst dashing along, those who had come along to watch the event were clearly having a whale of a time at the roadside Cafés and Trattorias.

We drove on to our hotel to join in the festivities at the bar, which didn't finish until around 3am, by which time we were absolutely shattered. The next morning, we awoke and went down for breakfast only to find out that the area of Emilia-Romagna in Northern Italy had suffered a magnitude 6.2 earthquake at around 5am, with a number of ancient buildings having collapsed in nearby towns, the very towns we had driven through and sadly many people had been killed. Guests had evacuated the hotel on hearing and feeling the earthquake, but my navigator and I were so exhausted that we didn't hear any commotion or feel any tremors and had slept through it all. My navigator turned to me at breakfast and said, "Did the earth move for you last night?", to which I hastily, just in case anyone was in earshot, and most firmly replied "No!".

Since taking part, the organisers have extended the duration of the event to four days, so that the race is primarily during daylight hours, which I think is a great shame. Also the event now involves all the entrants displaying their cars in the Piazza del Campo, no doubt to avoid anyone blocking the shop doorways! You might be surprised to learn that I don't think the Mille Miglia is the best historic rally in Europe, as it is more of a fast convoy than a competitive rally or race. However, the Mille Miglia is amazing and definitely an event to take part in at least once in your lifetime. It is noisy, full-on and generally chaotic from beginning to end. It is unlike anything you might have ever experienced in your life!

# TARGA FLORIO

*Volcanos & Tornados*

TARGA FLORIO

Distance: 700 miles over 3 days

Ferrari 330GT

Having immensely enjoyed the Mille Miglia the previous year, I decided to take part in the Targa Florio in Sicily during October, with another mate, in the hope of experiencing the full Italian "Road Racing" Job. The Targa Florio is the oldest sportscar racing event, originally taking place in 1906. Whilst it started out as a tour of the whole island, it was later restricted to a 45-mile circuit by the name of the Circuito Piccolo delle Madonie and was part of the World Sportscar Championship in 1955. It ran until 1977 when it was judged to be too dangerous to carry on. During its colourful history, many marques took part in the Targa Florio, in particular Healeys, which gained some success, and, prior to the event, I had seen the film "Mountain Legend" about the 1965 event. It was great to see so many clips of Healeys and their drivers, including a brief glimpse of Donald Healey's son Geoff. It is well worth a look!

My particular aspiration was to drive on the Madonie Circuit, which had once been graced by the likes of Nuvolari, Moss and Vaccarella among other famous racing drivers. In the early fifties, the event was, perhaps, predictably dominated by Italian entries, but nevertheless, a Healey Silverstone finished 16th overall out of 185 entries in 1950. A year in which the race was won by an Alfa Romeo 6C at an average speed of 54mph. During the year in which I participated the average speed was set at around 40mph.

Austin Healeys had some success late in the 1950's when a Healey Sprite finished 17th overall in 1959. I had considered taking part in my Austin

Healey 100, but eventually chose my old Ferrari, which had performed so well in the Mille Miglia. This subsequently turned out to be a particularly good decision, as you will discover when you read on.

Everyone was shocked to hear that the organisers of the Historic Targa Florio had gone bust a week before the event. All seemed lost and entrants were expounding their disappointment on Internet Forums, but thankfully for some, the Ferrari Factory came to the rescue and decided to take on the event, underwriting all costs (great PR exercise for its customers), but only for Ferrari owners! However, this didn't stop some keen enthusiasts from turning up in their Rileys and Alfas and the like, to simply follow the Ferrari event. It was a delight to see an Austin Healey 100 following on, with its numbers still in place from the previous year's event.

With my Ferrari Classiche Certificate in hand and having successfully passed scrutineering in a University car park in Palermo, we were given race number 10, and drove to the start in anticipation of a fairly easy first day's drive to Catania on the east coast. There were huge crowds in Palermo to see the cars leave, including many students from the University, which specialised in Engineering; an erudite bunch of spectators.

The route book took us via a coast road to Cefalu and then over the mountains to a closed road section on the slopes of Mount Etna. We were the third oldest Ferrari taking part in the event and were therefore close to the front of the field of around 80 in the Tribute, following a few cars which had been especially brought over from the Factory Museum in Maranello to take part.

The first day was turning out to be quite uneventful until, as the light started to fade, we arrived at the foot of Mount Etna with the fuel light coming on and a speed test to adhere to. We hadn't passed any petrol stations during the afternoon and no nearby petrol stations were indicated in the route book. In case you are wondering, I had filled up the car near the lunch stop, but the mountain sections proved to be rather thirsty and we had been looking for a petrol station for many miles, but to no avail. Anyway, having emptied a reserve emergency can of petrol into the tank, in the darkness, we proceeded up through the forests towards the summit of Mount Etna and prayed. As you might imagine, the needle on the fuel gauge would drop further as we were steadily going up the mountain, which was rather disconcerting.

Proceeding carefully back down on the other side of the mountain, I tried to avoid touching the accelerator, sometimes warily coasting, and our prayers were eventually answered as we arrived at a small Petrol Station with only a few drops remaining! It transpired that we were not the only entrants having a problem with fuel, as there was a ridiculously long queue to a single petrol pump on the forecourt, a sight not too dissimilar to that seen during the fuel crisis in the 1970's. Many competitors were actually pushing their cars to the pump. This was clearly an oversight on the part of the organisers, not to have highlighted the lack of any filling stations on such a long section.

The organisers had, in their wisdom, arranged for the Ferraris to be driven into the centre of Catania that evening, which turned out to be a total disaster. The road books were all but useless; there were horns going off everywhere, scooters running alongside the cars, all the boy racers following with Ferrari or Italian flags in tow and the Italian Police escort bikes trying to keep the participants on the right track and the spectators at bay. As I had previously experienced, in the best Italian tradition, it was total chaos!

The following day, after an early breakfast, we travelled along some fast road sections in the southern part of the island, where the roads were wide, perfectly smooth and almost entirely traffic free. The lunch stop was at the Castle of Chiaramonte in Agrigento on the southern coast, which is a UNESCO World Heritage Site, looking out over the Mediterranean. This was a wonderful location on the coast and a very civilised buffet lunch was had by all.

After lunch we headed back to Palermo, leaving the deep blue cloudless skies behind. From the pleasant 30-degree temperatures in Agrigento we were astonished to encounter, not just a summer storm, but a full-blown tornado en-route to Palermo! We faced torrential rain and strong gusting winds, as you might expect from a tornado, and with Central Palermo being flooded and many roads closed, the organisers had to swiftly find another route.

Apparently, there were some fatalities that afternoon, from boats capsizing off the coast. The weather was extreme to say the least, with volcanic ash falling everywhere and we experienced a mudslide at first hand, which resulted in our car coming to an abrupt halt. Emergency vehicles arrived and the road was soon closed to all traffic. Having ensured that no ash had breached the air filters and gone into the engine we ventured on into Palermo and spent the evening under the bonnet, in a large industrial unit taken over by a few of the other participants and their cars. A number of mechanics from the Ferrari Factory, carefully checked the cars and made sure that all was well. I was privileged to be given a complimentary set of red Ferrari factory overalls whilst messing around under the bonnet, so that I at least looked the part. Most of the participants did not experience what we, as one of the leading cars, had encountered. What a contrast from the serenity of the lunch stop!

The final day was a drive along the coast to Campofelice and onto the famous Madonie Circuit. After stopping at the old pits for some photos, and to stretch our legs and catch up with fellow competitors on the previous day's excitement, we were allowed onto the original circuit, where the roads were found to be in a very poor state of repair, with many sections having fallen away over the years. On occasions, you would see a convoy of vehicles slowing almost to crawling pace, to skirt around areas where the actual road had simply vanished. It was very precarious, with there being no barriers up on the mountain roads, but that didn't stop the participants from pushing their luck wherever possible. At one point, our car was in the middle of a small convoy of three cars, a car valued at £3.5million in front of us and a similar model valued at around £2million behind us. Had we been unfortunate enough to be sandwiched in a three-car shunt, on one of the blind bends or hairpins, there could well have been an infamous insurance claim!

Our lunch stop was in the centre of a small town, Castelbuono, high up in the mountains, where we were able to sample some of the splendid local fare. The Porcini were fabulous. After lunch, we continued on the circuit, eventually coming down to a fast section along the coast, where the cars could really push on. With a full tank of petrol and a straight section of road, which had been partly closed for the event, everyone went flat out with engines screaming at full revs. It was a fitting way to finish this historic circuit and quite a spectacle for the local Ferrari enthusiasts.

Despite the excitement of the tornado, mudslides, poor roads and almost running out of fuel on Mount Etna, we finished the event unscathed and enjoyed the awards ceremony party at a delightful vineyard. We were able to sample the local wines, knowing that we didn't have to drive back, as our cars were already on their way home in the car transporters and we would be flying back to London the following day. Overall, the event was put together at fairly short notice, so I suppose one should give the organisers a little slack.

It was quite a low-key affair, the highlight being, of course, driving the historic circuit, which was partly closed to traffic. The route was spectacular and, putting aside the weather, not too demanding on the cars. I'm sure that the event will continue to run in the future. If you get a chance to take part in the Targa Florio or just to visit Sicily, it is well worth the trip to see the Targa Florio Museum and to simply follow the old Madonie Circuit, but please take care and make sure you fill up before taking on Mount Etna.

# PICOS PYRENEES

*Quick Way Down*

*PICOS PYRENEES*

*Distance: 1,250 miles over 6 days*

*Austin Healey 100M*

In the early to mid 1950's, there were a few small rallies in Southern France, Spain and Portugal, which attracted many amateur entrants, including one or two cars from our own shores. Among others, were the Rallye de Lisbon, the Iberian Rallye and the Rallye Soleil. The Rallye Soleil was centred around Cannes and would sometimes head towards the dizzy heights of the Pyrenees. During the event in 1954, one Austin Healey 100 took part, finishing 1st in class and 15th overall. No doubt the rally proved to be a great testing ground for the new model.

Being one of the best results for an Austin Healey that year, I thought it would be appropriate to seek another class award in my Austin Healey 100, and so, it transpired that I took part in the inaugural run of the Picos to Pyrenees Rally, taking the overnight ferry from Portsmouth to Bilbao, to ensure that the car was in fine fettle for the pre-event scrutineering. At Bilbao, we took the opportunity to visit the splendid Guggenheim Museum, before the rally started the following morning. The Guggenheim, designed by Frank Gehry, was well worth the visit, with outstanding displays of modern and contemporary art, giving the competitors at bit of light cultural relief before the off.

The event was for cars built between 1919 and 1982, with no accompanying service vehicles permitted. The organisers had provided a tulip road book and marked maps and had arranged jogularity and regularity sections, together with driving tests at various private grounds. The scrutineering was uneventful and the camaraderie amongst the competitors, many of whom had been on the overnight ferry, was great. On leaving Bilbao at the start of the rally the following day, we quickly climbed through the hills of Cantabria and the stunning Rio de la Sia Valley and then into the heart of the Picos de Europa, which is locally known as “Little Switzerland”. At one of the time controls in Matienzo, we stopped, conveniently, at a typically Spanish local bar. The drivers were quick to order an espresso or two, whilst the navigators could enjoy a pint whilst marking up the road book with various different coloured pens to assist them with the timing on the route.

Soon we were back behind the wheel, and, as we climbed higher and higher, we found we were starting to go above the snow line. This rally took place in the late autumn, so some of the roads were already lined with deep snow on each side and were very icy, making negotiating the hairpins quite a delicate affair. There was little or no overtaking, with the various entrants giving each other a wide berth as we approached each twist and turn. This was particularly the case with the Jaguar Mark IX saloon we encountered, which was so wide, it didn’t give us any chance of getting past. It was a little frustrating to be held up at times, but as soon as we reached a suitable point to overtake him, we were able to push on. The great thing about this region, is that the roads are very well surfaced, the scenery is magnificent and there is hardly any traffic at all. In fact, throughout this rally we encountered little non-rally traffic, which meant that the organisers did not need to close the roads for some of the fast-timed sections. Throughout the Picos we passed Catalan Castles aplenty as we headed across the Sierra Pena Sagra to the magnificent Parador Fuente De, in the foothills of the Macizo Central. This was truly an amazing hotel high up in the Picos. Thankfully, there had been no accidents and all the cars were still in one piece.

The following day was similarly uneventful as we descended and headed further west towards Costa Verde and over the mountains of Leon. The views as we travelled through the National Parks were amazing and were highlighted by bright blue cloudless skies and glorious sunshine. After staying at the Parador Cervera de Pisuerga, we were given a well-earned rest from negotiating the acute twists and turns of the mountain passes of the previous two days, and we were able to enjoy the open plains, of Sierra Palencia, which meant that we could really open up the throttle. Some of the roads on this section were very wide, long and straight. You could have been forgiven for thinking we were driving in one of the southern states of America, as we pushed on.

At the halfway stage, all was going very well, and we were in second position in class, with few penalties, and were enjoying the banter with crews around us, all of whom were keen to check each other's times during various regularities. The road books were very well prepared, with little or no errors each day; the organisers had provided speed tables and ancillary maps and the marshalling was excellent, with some of the passage controls being in very remote locations. My experienced navigator was of the opinion that the organisers of this event had been the best he had ever come across.

The rally had been organised in the UK, and there was a good mixture of British marques in the event, including other Healeys, Rileys, Triumphs, MGs and Jaguars. There were also some lovely Porsches, Alfas and Mercedes among the foreign entries. This helped the crews during roadside repairs as, if you didn't have the required part, the likelihood was that someone else would have it. As is often experienced on mountain rallies, the brakes were taking a hammering and at many of the lunch stops, the crews were jacking up their cars to check and adjust the pads and discs.

On the penultimate day, we were travelling along the high passes of San Lorenzo through the breath-taking Sierra de la Demanda and then heading north across the Navarra plains, where I believe some of the popular Spaghetti Westerns of the 1960's were filmed. The scenery on this part of the rally was exceptionally stunning. We had an enjoyable evening meal at the spectacular Parador Sos del Rey Catolico, but the rally hadn't yet finished for the day, as the organisers had arranged some night sections, just in case we were not being challenged enough and, undoubtedly to tire us out before we encountered the Pyrenees.

Having earned my Private Pilot's Licence some 20 years previous, I had proudly recorded a number of vintage aircraft in my log book, including taking the controls of a Supermarine Spitfire T9, during which I successfully performed a couple of victory rolls over the English countryside. It had also been my pleasure to meet a fellow Bentley driver who had flown with the Battle of Britain Memorial Flight, and to chat with him about the Hawker Fury altimeter which was fitted in my own Bentley Tourer. However, I never thought I would be making an entry in my flight logbook on this rally, but you never know what is around the corner!

It was the last but one stage on the final day of the rally and we were pushing on in some of the highest peaks in the Pyrenees, mostly in fog and low cloud. We were lying third in class now and closing in on the crew who were just ahead of us. As such, every second counted. After enjoying the Col de la Pierre St Martin, one of the highest roads on the rally, which was well surfaced and had barriers, we headed west to proceed along a narrow road over the Col d'Erroymendi and then on towards an even smaller road over the Col Bagargui, which had been closed to traffic exclusively for the rally. This road was single track in places and very uneven. As mentioned, we were driving in and out of the clouds well above the tree line and the roads were wet and slippery, but with the road being otherwise closed, we pushed on and passed a few competitors along the way. My navigator advised me that as we were keeping good time, I could back off. I'm not sure if he felt that I was going too fast for the conditions, but it was a relief to slow down in such a precarious setting. However, no sooner had he told me to back off, than he changed his mind and said to push on as he had miscalculated the timing. I pushed down on the accelerator and immediately felt the back of the car lighten and swing slightly. I tried to hold the car in a straight line but before we knew it, we were off the road and airborne!!

Thankfully, the flight didn't last long, and we slid down the mountain sideways, shaking and rattling, and being in dense cloud, not knowing if we would suddenly go over an escarpment. The car came to an abrupt halt at a very steep sideways angle, so steep in fact, that when I eventually undid my harness and opened my door, I practically fell out.

So, having come to a halt and all the banging and crashing had stopped, there was an eerie silence, and our first thought was that, thankfully, we were

both still alive and apparently hadn't suffered any injuries. We both got out of the car and climbed wearily back up to the road. The competitor behind us had stopped to see if we were okay but, as we had no cuts or bruises, we waved him on and waited patiently for the rally recovery team to rescue us. When they arrived, they looked over the edge of the road shaking their heads and, with a sharp intake of breath, advised us that they did not have the equipment to recover our car, which was around a hundred feet down the slope. They suggested we contact a garage in St Jean which was just over the border in France. I didn't know the French word for winch, but called the garage anyway and tried to explain our predicament in my schoolboy French, to a bemused garage owner.

Soon the light began to fade and all the other rally cars had gone through, although we later discovered that three other cars had also come off the road on this stage. It was thought that I had most probably found some oil or mud on the road and lost the back end. Anyway, we decided to take shelter under the canopy of an old disused ski chalet. It was almost dark, starting to rain and there was no sign of the French Recovery Truck. In the distance, we could initially hear, and then see, a VW camper van slowly coming up the road. We waved them down and they graciously stopped for us. The occupants were an elderly French couple on their holidays, and they spoke a little English. Phew! I asked them to have a look at my car from the road, and to explain the situation to the garage in St Jean, so that they could bring a winch to haul the car back up onto the road. After making the phone call, the pair invited us into their camper van for a glass of Bordeaux and some Brie. My navigator and I turned to each other at this point and questioned whether we had indeed survived the plunge or whether we had died and gone to heaven.

Anyway, the garage truck eventually arrived and, in the darkness, with a huge spotlight and heavy-duty winch, hauled the car back onto the road. In order to do so, we had to move several boulders out of the way and in so doing, we established why the car hadn't rolled. It was evident that, having taken flight, we almost immediately landed, square, on top of a very large bolder which was held by the chassis of the car and kept us upright as we headed down the slope.

Once the car had been recovered and was back on the level, I started the engine. The oil pressure was fine, there were no petrol leaks, the tyres looked okay and all seemed fine, so we slowly proceeded back down the mountain, keeping to the road this time, to the finish.

At the end of the rally a gala Black-Tie dinner had been arranged at a swish hotel in San Sebastian. We parked our car outside the hotel with the other rally cars and ventured inside. The dinner was already in full swing. As you can imagine, we were wet and covered in mud and goodness knows what else from our adventure, and as we entered the double doors, the diners gave us a huge cheer and resounding applause, to recognise the fact that we had, against the odds, actually made it to the finish.

Despite getting full penalties for the last stage, we were not only classified as finishers, but we had managed to finish 6th in class for Pre-1960 cars, which was an amazing result. Not quite first place but I doubt that the Austin Healey which took part in the Rallye Soleil in 1954 took flight and went off a mountain. Anyway, we had finished, and more importantly, we were still in one piece.

# RALLY PREPARATION

*Foresight & Hindsight*

*RALLY PREPARATION*

*Foresight & Hindsight*

As you will have gathered, I am not a mechanic or an engineer and have very much learnt along the way, or literally on the roadside.

In this day and age, with the reliability of modern cars, and now particularly with electric cars, there are fewer things to go wrong, and so it is increasingly rare to find anyone who will even lift the bonnet, let alone undertake any mechanical work themselves. Many people outside the classic car fraternity, do not need to be bothered about checking the oil and water or possibly even the tyre pressures on their cars.

In the 1950's brand new cars would often break down, with some models being more notorious than others, and so owners were almost forced to take an interest in the upkeep of their cars. I well remember in the 1970's helping to bump start neighbours' cars, which were, in some cases, less than a year old. Therefore, driving cars which are now more than 60 years old, I suppose it is inevitable that they are likely to break down from time to time, due to wear and tear and the usual common failures. However, in my experience, accepting that old cars will let you down, sometimes at the most inconvenient moment, we just have to accept that it is all part of the fun.

They say, "A little knowledge is a dangerous thing"; however, I would say that, being backed up by reliable professionals, I have been able, with a little knowledge, to keep my cars up and running, allowing me to take part in many amazing events and adventures. If you make the effort to check under the bonnet now and again, before attempting any serious rallies, you will have half a chance of knowing what you are looking at and understanding what needs doing, when the need arises.

Unless you are a capable mechanic, you will also need to employ a specialist garage to ensure that your car is in fine fettle before any rally. It is essential to find a competent and trustworthy repair shop, with whom you can build up a good working relationship. Thankfully, I have discovered a few great local mechanics in whom I can place my trust, and with whom I have become very good friends over the years.

I am not qualified to give a detailed account on vehicle preparation, but would recommend that you do not take too many spares, unless you have a support vehicle, as more often than not, there is seldom time to do anything more than a quick make-do-and-mend between controls. If you do encounter anything serious, hopefully you will be able to find a local garage with facilities to assist and, if need be, have parts flown out. I recall on the Alpine Rally one year, a competitor having some half shafts flown out, so that they could re-join the rally a few days later. There have been a few occasions when I have been thankful for having in the boot, some copper wire, duct tape, WD40 and a clothes peg or two! Not that this should be condoned, but I recall borrowing some wire from a farmer's fence, somewhere in France, on one trip and I'm pretty certain I didn't return to replace it.

It is not wise to ignore the serviceability of the standard equipment on your car, such as suspension, tyres, wipers, brakes etc, as some rallies only offer limited recovery and support. For most rallies it will be compulsory to carry warning triangles, first aid kit, fire extinguisher, hi-viz jackets and spare bulbs.

On some rallies, you may encounter very rough roads and so you might consider protecting the exhaust or, as is the case with my Austin Healey 100, you just need to learn to drive more slowly. A skid plate on the leading edge of the silencer may be a worthwhile exercise. I welded plates to the base of the sump and the fuel tank of my Austin Healey, to prevent any damage from rocks and stones. You need to bear in mind though, that fitting a sump guard may result in the need for an oil cooler due to the guard's shielding of cooling air over the sump. You may also wish to fit a roll cage for added protection, a full three-point harness or at least good seatbelts, although I am not sure they would protect you if you were to go airborne on a mountain road. In addition, you might consider exchanging the dynamo for an alternator and generally overhauling the electrics, which invariably deteriorate over time, and perhaps install some spotlights, which are particularly useful for the night stages when you find yourself in the back of beyond.

Apart from allowing for breaking down, you also need to have a great navigator with whom you have a good rapport. This will ensure that you don't get lost too often, as they will carefully prepare the route book by marking up tricky turnings, locations of controls and tests and noting possible refuelling points etc. Preparation is key, as without it, when the crew starts to tire, errors can creep in. The golden rule, whenever there is any doubt on the route, is to stop and check the route book again, rather than having the embarrassment of driving along a road for some 30 miles only to find that you took the wrong turning. You may find it hard to turn around and get back on track. Everyone gets lost at some stage, but the difference between a successful crew and an ineffective one, is mostly to do with the speed with which a mistake is discovered and rectified.

To assist your navigator, it is recommended that you fit a decent flexible interior light and, if you are getting really serious, a magnifying Poti to help him or her to read the Ordnance Survey maps. In many of the rallies I have taken part in, I have used a mechanical Halda Tripmaster or Twinmaster (although Brantz units are equally as good). These are driven from the speedo cable, which, along with a good stopwatch, such as a Heuer which looks good on the dash, can be used with the car trip to confirm distances and times accurately.

You don't need to be an Olympic athlete, but it does pay to be fit on these rallies, in order to take on several days of non-stop competition. Quite often, accidents occur due to tiredness or overzealous driving. I would strongly recommend a few early nights, prior to the events and not indulging in too much alcohol until after the rally has finished, although you may recall that there were occasions in this book, where we ignored our own good advice and took advantage of the bar after a hard day's driving.

I have competed in many other European competitive rallies, beyond those mentioned in this book, with differing degrees of success, including the Enstall Classic in Austria. There are also the popular Classic Marathon and the London to Lisbon Rally, but these do not, in my opinion, have such a historical relevance to those rallies which were run in the 1950's. I have also competed in the fabulous Cento Ore, which is implemented along very similar lines to the historic Tour de France Automobile or Tour Auto, as it's known today, although the Cento Ore, as the name would suggest, takes place in Italy, and leads you to some great circuits such as Vallelunga and Imola. If you simply want to take part in a competitive event, regardless of its historic standing, then the Cento Ore arguably offers all the fun and more, compared with many of the retrospective rallies held today.

Taking part in the Porsche Club GB Speed Championship in the 1990's in my 993RS, at many circuits around the UK, and also a few forays into Europe, to compete on the famous circuits at Spa Francorchamps and Le Mans, was great fun. However, at such race circuits, the scenery gets rather samey after a few laps and it's a pain having to dice with others to keep the racing line, especially when some competitors may have tweaked and modified their cars, so that they can shoot past at will. Historic and Club racing is rarely a level playing field, despite the efforts of the organisers. In my opinion, circuit racing doesn't offer the same even-handedness or the thrills and spills you experience when taking part in historic rallies.

Before taking on any of the illustrious events mentioned in this book, I would strongly recommend that you join a local Rally Club and take part in some competitive runs nearer to home. You will find that Club members will be keen to give you tips on different motorsport regulations applied to the different events, the safety equipment required, which can differ from one rally to another and, most importantly, advice specifically relevant to your own car.

I remember taking part in a few Twelve Car Rallies in the UK before diving into the historic rally scene. They are held on public roads and are a good way of learning about, and practising, map reading, and also understanding regularities, passage controls and time controls. They may take place over an afternoon or evening and are very popular. One of my funniest experiences on these rallies, was when all twelve cars set off in an orderly fashion, in two-minute intervals, and all turned left half a mile down the road. After re-reading the instructions, it became apparent to everyone that we should have turned left around 100 yards from the start. The resulting chaos, with all twelve cars swerving around each other, tyres squealing, drivers pulling over to recalibrate their trip meters and navigators trying to recalculate the times, was hilarious. How could the entire rally go so wrong, so soon? I'm still not sure why the organisers just didn't allow everyone to re-start the stage.

When taking part in any of the retrospective historic rallies, the idea is to lose as few penalty points as possible. This can be achieved by ensuring you don't run out of petrol by having a Jerry can in the boot, keeping on the pace, always checking the control times properly and noticing any errors by marshals when completing your timecard. Incidentally, it pays to be pleasant and courteous to the marshals! In short, you need to simply focus upon your own efforts rather than trying to push yourself to catch up with the car in front.

Finally, don't forget, as one old competitor once said to me, in order to finish first, first you have to finish!

MILLE MIGLIA
TARGA FLORIO
ALPINE
LIEGE-ROME
TULIP

Lightning Source UK Ltd.
Milton Keynes UK
UKHW022021051120
372857UK00006B/156/J